# Silly Sketcher

# Draw Funny Bugs!

written by **Luke Colins**

illustrated by **Catherine Cates**

**BLACK
RABBIT
BOOKS**

Hi Jinx is published by Black Rabbit Books
P.O. Box 3263, Mankato, Minnesota, 56002.
www.blackrabbitbooks.com
Copyright © 2020 Black Rabbit Books

Jennifer Besel, editor; Catherine Cates,
interior designer; Michael Sellner, cover designer;
Omay Ayres, photo researcher

Library of Congress Cataloging-in-Publication Data
Names: Colins, Luke, author.
Title: Draw funny bugs! / by Luke Colins.
Description: Mankato, Minnesota : Black Rabbit Books, [2020] |
Series: Hi jinx. Silly sketcher | Includes bibliographical references and
index. | Audience: Age 8-12. | Audience: Grade 4 to 6.
Identifiers: LCCN 2018008941 (print) | LCCN 2018010252 (ebook) |
ISBN 9781680729542 (e-book) | ISBN 9781680729481 (library binding) |
ISBN 9781644660737 (paperback)
Subjects: LCSH: Insects—Caricatures and cartoons—Juvenile literature. |
Cartooning—Technique—Juvenile literature. Classification:
LCC NC1764.8.I57 (ebook) | LCC NC1764.8.I57 C65 2020 (print) |
DDC 741.5/1—dc23
LC record available at https://lccn.loc.gov/2018008941

Printed in China. 1/19

## Image Credits

Alamy: Matthew Cole, 2-3, 5; iStock: carbouval, 5; Shutterstock: Luciano
Cosmo, Cover; Mario Pantelic, Cover, Back Cover, 3, 5; Memo Angeles,
Cover, 5, 8, 12, 15, 16, 18, 20, 23; mohinimurti, 19; Olga Sabo, 5;
opicobello, 7, 8, 17; owatta, 5; Pasko Maksim, Back Cover, 14, 17, 23, 24;
Pitju, 3, 21; Ron Dale, 3, 4, 5, 6, 8, 14, 20; Tueris, 14; VectorArtFactory, 20
Every effort has been made to contact copyright holders for material
reproduced in this book. Any omissions will be rectified in subsequent
printings if notice is given to the publisher.

# Contents

# Chapter 1

# Be a Silly Sketcher!

Insects are wiggly, silly little things. But when you give them big eyes and crazy situations, the laughs will be loud.

To be a silly sketcher, all you need is a pencil, some paper, and a funny bone. Draw an oval here. Put a rectangle there. Add some lines or squiggles. Just follow the steps. You'll have hilarious drawings in no time.

# What You Need

pencils

pencil sharpener
(just in case)

lots of paper    eraser

colored pencils and markers

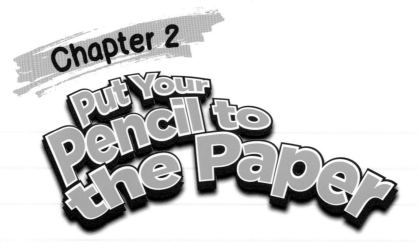

## Chapter 2
## Put Your Pencil to the Paper

Let's start with a simple sketch to get the giggles going. Draw a caterpillar trying to stay on a branch, and try not to laugh!

### Step 1
Start with two long, curved lines.

### Step 2
Draw a wavy body around the lines. Add in two eye circles.

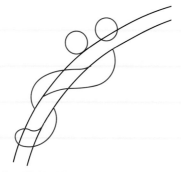

### Step 3
Add details, such as **antennae** and tiny curved legs.

## Step 4

Erase all the lines inside the **overlapping** shapes.

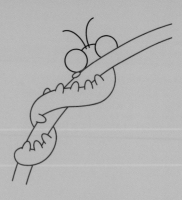

## Step 5

Give your caterpillar pupils, a little mouth, and details on its body.

## Step 6

Add **motion** lines and a few more body details.

## Finish It Up!

Use markers to outline your drawing. Then try colored pencils for shading it in.

# Dizzy Dragonfly

After drawing this dragonfly, you might be dizzy with laughter!

## Step 1

Start the body by layering a small oval, a teardrop, and a long skinny oval.

## Step 2

Draw big oval wings. Give the dragonfly circle eyes and body details.

## Tip

Your dragonfly doesn't have to be dizzy. Try giving it a different **emotion**.

## Step 3

Add silly legs and a mouth.

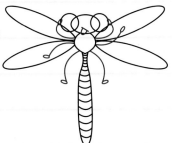

## Step 4

Erase all the lines inside the overlapping shapes.

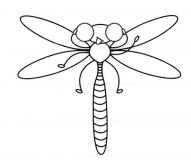

## Step 5

Use swirls and squiggle lines to make your bug dizzy.

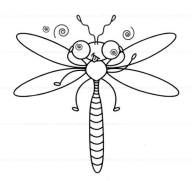

## Step 6

Add motion lines.

# Bumbling Bee

Bee creative! Sketch this silly bug
falling out of your favorite flower.

## Step 1
Start the plant by
drawing a Y shape.

## Step 2
Add in leaves.
Maybe take a
bite out of one!

## Step 3
Start the bee's body
with ovals and
squiggle lines.

## Step 4
Draw in funny
legs and eyes.

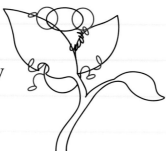

## Step 5

Erase all the lines inside the overlapping shapes.

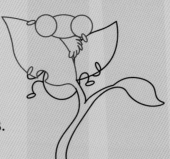

## Step 6

Add wings and antennae. Don't forget the stinger!

## Step 7

Finish the bee's face.

## Step 8

Add detail to the leaves. Draw in motion lines too.

# Butt Bright

Is there anything funnier than a bug with a light-up butt? Make your firefly extra bright.

## Step 1

Use rounded shapes to start the body.

## Step 2

Add big eyes and wings. Draw a little mouth too.

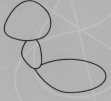

## Step 3

Erase all the lines inside the overlapping shapes.

## Step 4
Give your firefly antennae,
arms, and legs.

## Step 5
Add pupils, little hands,
and body details.

## Step 6
Draw in tiny feet and
eyebrows. Finish
the antennae.

## Step 7
Add lines to make
your firefly shine.

13

# Lovely Lady

The spotted beetles kids love are called by many names. Some people call them ladybugs. Others call them ladybirds or lady beetles. Let's just call this one fun.

### Step 1
Start the head and the body.

### Step 2
Add eyes, arms, legs, and antennae.

### Step 3
Add details, such as hands and shoes.

If you have trouble making the shapes, try **tracing** them first. Tracing is a good way to get a feel for how to draw something. Then try it on your own.

## Step 4
Erase all the lines inside
the overlapping shapes.

## Step 5
Draw the ladybug's spots.
Add a mouth too.

## Step 6
Add pupils and eyebrows.
Start the purse.

## Step 7
Finish the sketch with
more details.

# Fly Swatter

This drawing puts a fly in a tricky situation.

## Step 1

Draw a wavy rectangle to start the flyswatter. Start the head and eyes too.

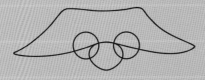

## Step 2

Add **horizontal** lines to the flyswatter. Draw in a crushed **proboscis**.

## Step 3

Put in **vertical** lines on the swatter. Add a handle too.

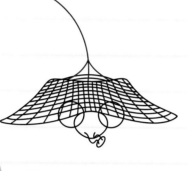

## Step 4

Give the fly some arms and legs.

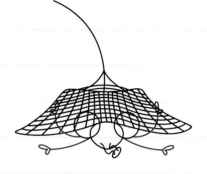

## Step 5

Erase all the lines inside the overlapping shapes.

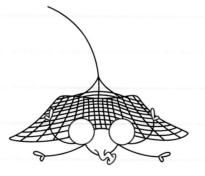

## Step 6

Add details, such as motion lines.

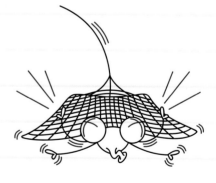

**Tip**

Try drawing in a scene. Maybe the fly is on a kitchen table.

# Hungry Mosquito

A mosquito ready for dinner will make anyone laugh.

### Step 1
Use ovals and circles to start the mosquito's body.

### Step 2
Use wavy lines for the legs, arms, chest, and antennae.

### Step 3
Add in wings and a long proboscis.

## Step 4

Erase all the lines inside the overlapping shapes.

## Step 5

Give your hungry bug a bib. Add body detail too.

## Step 6

Draw in some mischievous eyes and a mouth.

## Step 7

To be funny, give the bug a tongue and silverware.

## Step 8

Finish the sketch with motion lines. Put a joke on the bib.

# Chapter 3
## Get in on the Hi Jinx

Professional animators use the same steps you just did! They use simple shapes to build the frames of their drawings. Then they add details, such as shading and color. Maybe one day you'll make a cartoon about bugs!

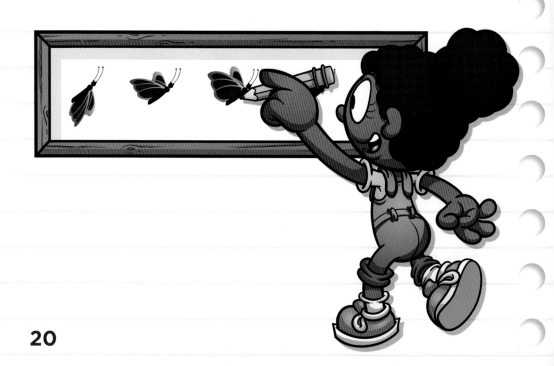

# Take It One Step More

1. Most of the drawings tell you to erase the lines inside overlapping shapes. Why should you do that?

2. Are your sketches more or less funny with color? Why?

3. What features make these drawings funny?

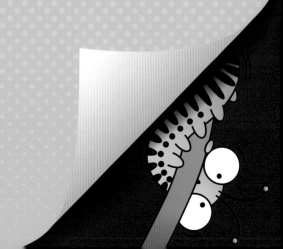

# GLOSSARY

**antenna** (ahn-TEN-uh)—one of a pair of skinny organs on the heads of insects

**emotion** (e-MOH-shun)—a state of feeling

**horizontal** (hor-uh-ZON-tuhl)—being parallel to the horizon

**motion** (MO-shun)—an act or process of moving

**outline** (AHWT-lyn)—to draw a line around the edges of something

**overlap** (oh-vur-LAP)—to extend over or past

**proboscis** (prah-BAH-sis)—a long, thin tube that is part of an insect's mouth

**trace** (TRAYS)—to copy something by following the lines or letters as seen through a transparent sheet on top

**vertical** (VUR-tuh-kuhl)—straight up and down

## BOOKS

**Bergin, Mark.** *Draw Birds.* Step-by-Step. Mankato, MN: Book House, 2019.

**Johnson, Clare.** How to Draw. New York: Dorling Kindersley Limited, 2017.

*Let's Draw Animals with Crayola!* Crayola. Minneapolis: Lerner Publications, 2018.

## WEBSITES

Drawing for Kids
**mocomi.com/fun/arts-crafts/drawing-for-kids/**

How to Draw
**www.hellokids.com/r_12/drawing-for-kids/**

How to Draw Archive
**www.artforkidshub.com/ how-to-draw/**

# TIPS AND TRICKS

Colored pencils are a great tool for coloring in your drawings. Layer a color over another for a cool blended effect.

Can't draw a straight line? Try using a ruler or other straight edge.

Don't worry if your drawings don't look exactly like the ones in this book! Art is all about creating your own thing. Just have fun!

If you're having trouble, look at pictures of the real bugs. That might inspire you!